Made in the USA
Middletown, DE
19 August 2021

46350976R00057